SHORT STORIES AND ESSAYS

By Arnold C.J. Burks

CONTENTS

Short Stories

Essays

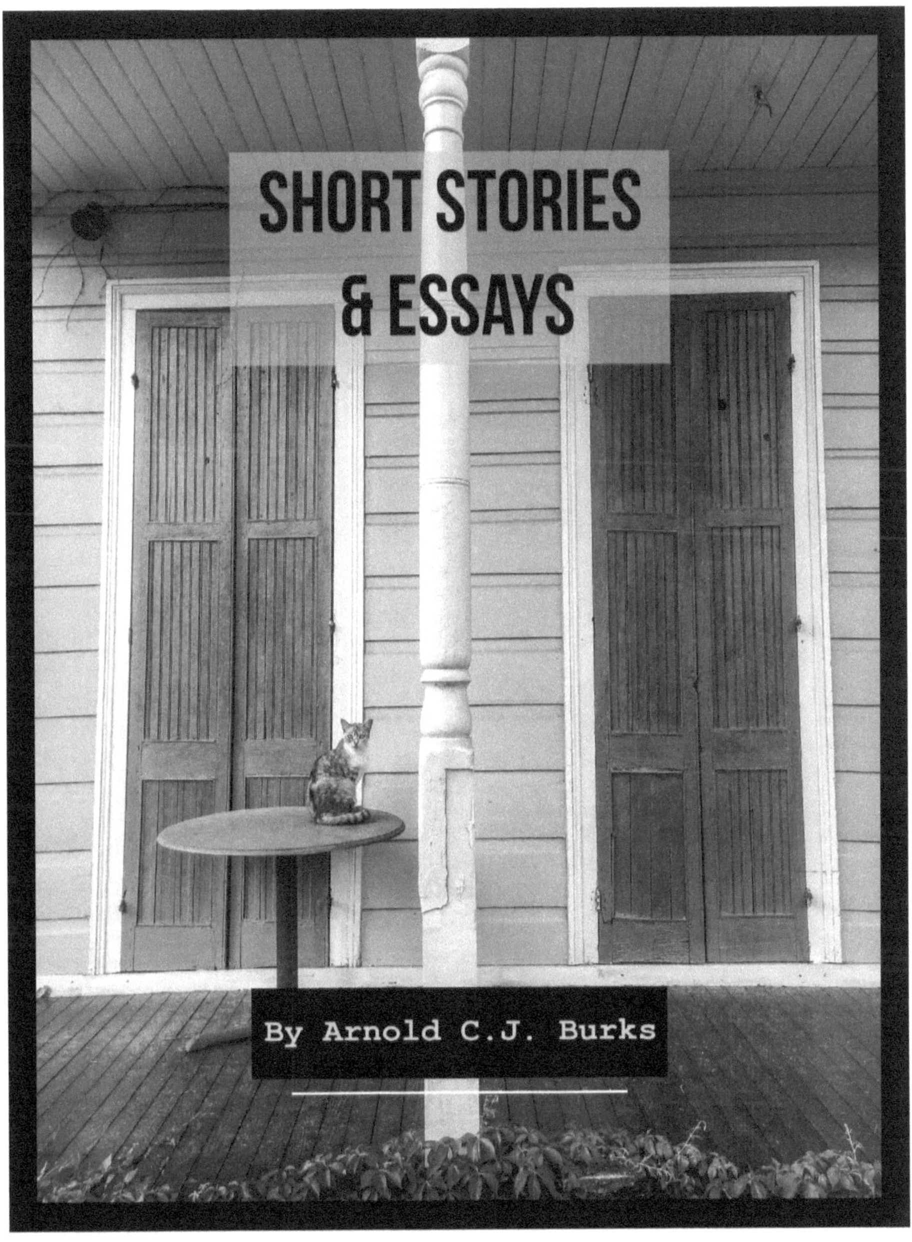
SHORT STORIES
& ESSAYS
By Arnold C.J. Burks

For Rosanna, Mommy…

WHO DAT CALLED DA' POLICE?

Momma was still at work. I wanted to wait until she got off to do my homework, but I knew she was gon' be tired. My momma be always mad, especially when she come home and the front room dirty with our toys and stuff. So when the after school van dropped me and my sister Julie off at home, I told her we had to clean up before momma got off. I put on the same shirt I always see momma wear when she clean up on Saturdays. It fit me too big though. I made Julie a bowl of cereal, and she ate while I cleaned up.

Every morning my momma wake up at 5:30 and go to her first job. It's my job to wake up by 6:45, get Julie out of bed, make sure we brush our teeth, eat our cereal, and have on our uniform by time momma make it back home to bring us to school. Our school is only 'bout four blocks away, but momma said we too young to walk by our self.

It was 4:30 in the evening now and momma was getting off at 5, but she wouldn't be home 'til 5:30. Julie fell asleep on the couch. I miss being in kindergarten like her 'cause we ain't never had homework. I like first grade, but we don't get no naps and I used to tell momma that big boys don't need naps but I don't feel that way nomo'. Julie learned how to stop, drop, 'n roll at school today. For homework she had to read this sheet about how to call

911 when issa' emergency. They had a fireman and a fire truck on it, and she had to color it. But she fell asleep doing it. That's my sister.

My daddy always tell us to color in between the lines. I like when we go spend the weekend with daddy, but I hate when him and momma fuss. I hope they don't be fussing over me and Julie.

I heard somebody knock at the door, and I walked slowly to peak out the window. I ain't want nobody to know we was home 'cause momma say children ain't supposed to be home by they self. We could get in trouble for it, but we ain't got no choice. My maw-maw died last year right after Tupac died, and my auntie been in the hospital, so we ain't had nobody to watch us while mommy and daddy at work. One night after momma put me and Julie to bed, I heard her crying in the kitchen, and I went in there to rub her back like she always do when I be crying. I stayed up with her even though it was a school night.

When I peeked out the window, I saw it was Armani. I waved and opened the door.

"Hey Johnny, you done your homework?"

"Almost, I gotta clean up before my momma get home."

She told me everybody was outside playing basketball and jumping rope 'cause they was done with they homework. I said I might come out there when my momma got off. She said bye and I watched her walk back up the street. One day at school, Kevin told me Armani told him she like me. She cute. I like when her momma put her hair in Afro Puffs, and I like when she wear them pink barrettes.

When I closed the door and turned around, all I saw was Julie holding the house phone in her hand, and the bowl of cereal spilled on the carpet. I was mad because I had another mess to clean up before momma got home. Even worse, the milk got onto my homework. I heard a voice on the phone and I grabbed it out of Julie's hand. The lady on the other line said, "Officers are on the way, okay?" I hung up the phone and yelled at Julie. All she said was, "I'm saw-wee. I was doing my homework."

It was 5:02. Momma was off, and would be home soon. I got a

towel and grabbed a chair to stand on so I could reach the sink. I wet the towel, and rushed over to the carpet to clean up the mess. Five minutes later I heard a knock on the door, and a voice said "Police!" I didn't know what to do. I just thought of momma being mad at me. I opened the door, and saw two police officers. They didn't say nothing at first, just looked around at the inside of the living room, probably noticing the crayons and cereal on the ground. Me and Julie both wearing nothing but momma shirts made them look at us even more crazier. They was white too. They didn't ask to come in our nothing.

"Uhh, somebody here called 911?" one of them said.

"Sorry sir, that was a assadent. My sister learned about how to stop, drop, 'n roll today at school and she was doing her home-work on how to dial 911 and she assadently called y'all by mis-take."

I saw everybody in the neighborhood looking at us. The chil-dren who was playing basketball and jumping rope stopped and started whispering. All the grown-ups was peeking out they win-dows at us. Nosy asses. Ms. Pierre's son, Manny, was pitching rocks at the abandoned house next door to us. Every time he did it, it sounded like it could've been a gun shot or something.

"Hey! Put the fucking rocks down" the other cop said.

His name was Officer Gregory. Daddy told me always read a officer name tag in case something happen. Manny just looked at him and kept pitching the rocks at the house. All the other big teenagers walked toward the abandoned house, and just sat there, like they was waiting for the police to do something. I could tell Officer Gregory wanted to do something to them, but the other one, Officer Parsons, told him to calm down.

"Okay. Are your parents home?" asked Officer Parsons.

"Yeah my momma is, but she in the tub. She just got off work."

I was lying. I didn't want look up at the sky 'cause I know my maw-maw probably sitting next to God shaking her head at me. But if she was here right now I wouldn't have to lie. I'm sorry maw-maw. I'm sorry God.

"Alright. Y'all be careful with that telephone from now on. We have to respond to emergencies only, okay?"

"Yes sir."

As soon as they turned they backs, I shut the door and locked it. I went to the window and watched as Officer Gregory approached the boys at the abandoned house. He pointed across the street, demanding them to move. They just stared at him. One of them spit on the ground, not far from his shoe. But when Officer Parsons came at them, they moved, still looking at the cops dirty.

Soon as the police got in the car and pulled off, Manny and them went and sat back down by the abandoned house.

It was 5:25 now, and I knew momma would walk through the door any minute. I rushed to clean up. I never cleaned up so fast in my whole life. Julie helped me. I didn't use the vacuum or the broom though 'cause I'm too short.

Momma walked through the door at 5:31. Me and Julie was acting like we was reading. Julie's book was upside down, but I don't think momma noticed.

"Hey ma!"

"Hey my babies, y'all finished ya' homework?"

"Yeah!"

After she changed clothes, she started cooking. I went outside and played with Armani and 'nem. Julie stayed inside and watched Scooby Doo. One of the old women across the street asked if everything was okay at our house. I said "yea" and kept walking. Momma said she nosy, always asking too many questions.

Once the sun started going down I went back inside and took my bath. Momma made Sloppy Joes. I ate mines with fries, and Julie fell asleep on the couch after she ate half of hers. Momma woke her up and told her to go lay down in bed.

"We going see daddy this weekend Ma?"

"Yeah. On Friday, after school."

I got beaucoup excited. "Thank you Ma."

"For what?"

"For everything."

She smiled, and walked toward the house phone. She started

scrolling through the call log, but I wasn't paying attention. I put my plate in the sink, and sat on the couch.

"Johnny, who called 911 today?"

FRANKIE CAN'T READ

I walked outside the gate to wait for the pickup van after school. Chris was out there with his Pokémon cards, sitting on the ground with some dude with a small 'fro. I sat down next to Chris and said "Boy I'll jack your cards." The dude sitting next to him said "You ain't gon' jack nothing while I'm right here." Chris smiled and said "Yea, you ain't gon' jack nothing while Frank right here." Frank stared at me and said "Go head, I dare ya." He musta' thought I was tryna' bully Chris or something. What he didn't know was that it's a game we play, me and Chris. If I'm out here with my cards first, he say "Ima jack you" then sit next to me. We be trading cards but we don't know what we be doing. We just be guessing which Pokémon be better than the other one.

Chris was being messy instead of telling Frank to be cool. "I'm just playing with him dawg" I said. Chris laughed and said "Boy you a whole hoe." Frank gave Chris dap, then started to stand up. "Y'all boys be cool" he said, and started walking down the street. After he walked off, I knocked the cards out Chris' hands. He ain't care, he just kept laughing.

"You down bad dawg. Where that boy from?"

"The 4th Ward I think."

I saw Frank make a left on Carrollton and start walking toward Canal Street.

A week later, I went to use the bathroom on the third floor at school, even though I was supposed to go to the one on the second floor. I be wanting Isabella to see me up there so she'll think I'ma fifth grader like her. Soon as I walked in the bathroom I saw Frank, standing with some fifth graders. He looked at me, but I put my head down buku quick and walked to the urinal. I swear I thought he was gon' sneak me while my back was turned, and they was gon' jump me. Dawg, I never pissed for so long in my life. Usually it only take like 15 seconds, tops, for me to be done. But I had all that Hawaiian Punch at lunch. Just my luck. I held my pants down with one hand, and balled my other hand up into a fist. If they swung at me, I was gon' turn around buku quick with my pants down and piss on them boys. Nobody did me nothing though. After I washed my hands, Frank said "Wuzam Calvin" and gave me dap. "My bad 'bout the other day. I was just tryna' protect Chris. He told me people be messin' with him in his class. My momma know his momma, and she told me to look out for him." That was true. Chris told me Mike be hating on him because Angela like him. I had buku fights with Mike last year, but not nomo' because we ain't in the same class.

"It's all gravy dawg" I told him.

"Who class you in?" Frank asked.

"Mrs. Rene, you in Mrs. Aguillard class ha?"

"Yea. With her fine ass." Everybody in the bathroom bussed out laughing.

Me and Frank walked into the hall, talking. Next thing you know, Isabella walked out her classroom. "Wuzam Isabella" Frank said. I looked at him confused, and waited on Isabella to embarrass him. "Hey Frankie" she said, and walked towards us. Her smile so pretty, bruh. Chris be calling her Spanish just 'cause she red and her hair kinda straight and her people from…Poortoe Rica or Damen-nigga Public, one of 'em. I told him she Black 'cause my daddy told me they had slavery on the islands too. She look like she could be Mrs. Aguillard's daughter, even though Mrs. Aguillard Creole. They both look alike.

"This my potna Calvin ya heard me."

"Wassup Calvin" Isabella said, looking at me for the first time in my life.

"Wuzam?" I said, all cool. Every year since I was in Kindergarten, me, Isabella, and five other students took a group picture to-gether for student of the month. Last year we did it THREE times. And she ain't noticed me until now. Women bruh...

Her and Frankie talked for like two more minutes but I wasn't listening, just staring at her eyes, neck, everything. I ain't start listening again until she told Frank "Class be boring without you". Frank was in 4th grade like me, so that didn't make sense seeing as how Isabella was a grade above us.

When she walked off I asked "Boy how you know her?" He laughed and said "We was in the same class last year. But I got kept back 'cause I ain't pass the LEAP test." When he saw I didn't believe him he said "I just turned 11 son, like a man. I was born in '91." All school year the teachers been going crazy about the LEAP, but I ain't worried 'bout it. Mrs. Rene got frustrated with me one day when she was tryna' teach me my times tables, and told me I was gon' fail. I told my momma and she said "We gon' show that white hoe, you gon' do more than pass. That paper gon' say MASTERY or ADVANCED."

Me and Frankie grew to be real cool with each other. It's crazy how that turned out. We started playing ball together after school while I waited for the pickup van to come. About a month later, we started LEAP practice. They put me, Chris, and Frankie, all in the same class. Mrs. Rene let us sit by each other, and that was where she messed up at. On the last day of practice, she made Chris read a paragraph in the workbook out loud.

"Woahh, it's me."

"What? Where do you see that at?" Mrs. Rene looked at the workbook. "Chris, this says Woe is me." The class bussed out laughing. You could see Mrs. Rene face turning red, and I tried to hide my face so she couldn't see me laughing. I'm so goofy, Chris could tell a joke, and I'ma still be giggling two hours later. An-gela was laughing the loudest, and I could tell Mike hatin' ass was burnt up.

Mrs. Rene made me read next, and it sounded like I was bouta cry while I was reading 'cause I was tryna' hold my laughter in. "Goofy ass" Frankie said, shaking his head at me. While Mrs.

Rene had her back turned, Mike threw a piece of paper at Chris, and it popped him upside the head. All Chris scary ass said was "Chill bruh." Frankie told Mike "Stop playing with him", and Mike looked at Frankie crazy, but ain't say nothing. Frankie was the tallest dude in class, and everybody knew he was older than us now. So Mike knew he couldn't punk Frankie how he be doing Chris.

I never had trouble reading, my problem always been math. I swear, if all I had to do in class everyday was read, I would be in college right nah. Frankie had to read next. I was still giggling at Chris' joke, and Mrs. Rene told me to stop laughing, but I couldn't. When Frankie opened his mouth, he stuttered on the first word. "T-T-T-T-T-T…" was all he could get out. The whole class bussed out laughing. "QUIET" yelled Mrs. Rene. Everybody kept laughing, Chris fell on the floor, and I had to stick my head under the desk so she couldn't see me. It really felt like tears was 'bouta come out my eyes. Mrs. Rene said "Terror, sweetie" and Frankie repeated the word. He struggled with that same sentence for the next 30 seconds. My stomach hurt from laughing so much, it felt like I had six pack abs.

"Man he can't read" said Mike. I picked my head back up, and saw Frankie staring at the workbook, with a confused look on his face. The whole time I thought he was playing. "Old ass, no wonder he up in here with us" said Mike. The class started laughing again, but it wasn't funny to me nomo'. "Boy I'll sneak you" said Frankie, and stood up. Mike told him "I wouldn't even fight you dawg. I'ma just chase you round the school with a book." Everybody was crying laughing at that point, and I didn't know how Mrs. Rene was gon' get ahold of the class. Last time something like this happened, she started crying and ran to the principal's office by herself.

After that, my memory ain't too clear. All I remember was Chris told Mike something, and Mike snuck him. Next thing you know I was on top of Mike, workin' his ass. Everybody said he grabbed some scissors off the floor, that must be how I got this gash on my arm, and Frankie jumped in and grabbed the scissors from him. But all the teachers saw when they broke up the fight was me swinging on Mike, and Frankie kneeling over him, holding scissors. Mike told them we jumped him.

The news people came to the school with cameras and everything. The whole neighborhood was crowded around the fence, tryna see what was going on. I didn't understand what the big fuss was about. The police came and questioned me too, but I told them I didn't know nothing. Mrs. Rene was crying and running her mouth to the police like she was the one got stabbed or something. But I ain't care 'bout the police coming to school. I was mad they called my momma. She had to leave work and catch the bus all the way to the school.

"Dawg I'm tired of being in the fourth grade. I don't want get kept back again" Frankie told me while we were in the lobby, sitting outside the principal's office. He was staring at the ground. He looked scared. I could see my momma and Mike momma talking to the principal inside the office. Well, my momma wasn't saying much. Mike momma was doing all the talking. I couldn't hear what she was saying though. I looked behind me and saw people in the hallway, walking past the lobby, pointing and staring at us. Isabella was out there too. When she saw me looking she waved. I nodded my head and she smiled. Women weird bruh...

I was about to tell Frankie about the girls staring at us, but I could tell he wouldn't care. Mike momma came out of the office and walked straight to the door, didn't even look at us. My momma shook hands with Principal Gasper as they walked out of the office. I braced myself, ready to get fussed at. Luckily, I had one of them mommas who didn't believe in giving her children whippins' in public. So I ain't have to worry 'bout that until we got home. "C'mon baby" she said. That was it? I couldn't believe it. I dapped Frank off and started walking with my momma. Before we walked out of the school, I looked back and saw Principal Gasper standing over Frankie, who was still staring at the ground. My momma grabbed my attention when she said "I love you Calvin." I turned toward her and said "I love you too ma", then we walked out of the door.

BUDDY'S DEAD

Buddy was dead. The star basketball player at our school. Our whole team was sitting in the hallway, silent. If somebody had to drop a tear, they put the collar of their shirt over their face so nobody would see them sobbing. Coach Smooth (his real name was Coach Wallace, but his nickname in high school was Smooth 'cause of the way he handled the ball on the court) was in his office, on the phone with Buddy's parents.

"Uptown 'bout to be extra hot" Reed said. Theo smacked his teeth and said "Man you know damn well whoever did that shit wasn't from Uptown." The hallway got quiet again. Reed was right, to a certain extent. No matter who did it, and where the killer was from, Buddy being killed Uptown was gonna make the police patrols more heavy than they already were.

Buddy was the typical wild and crazy red nigga from the 7th Ward. Never backed down from nothing and nobody. That's what made him such a good basketball player. He had a lot of heart. One time at a party, Buddy got into an argument with some dudes from the 6th Ward, and it seemed like it wasn't their first argument. But at the end of the day, nobody knew who did it for sure, 'cause Buddy lived a whole different life when he left school and went back home. His hood been at war for years. People thought things would change after Katrina hit two years ago, but nah...

It was 9:15 A.M., and we were supposed to be in our first period by now, but Principal Dixon told us we could be together and grieve. Once I saw Mr. Martin walking up the hallway towards us,

I took it that Principal Dixon didn't let him know. "Matthew, why aren't you in my class?" he said to me. "Umm…" was all I could muster up. Mr. Martin was an old man, but his senses were quick, and he didn't hunch over when he walked. He was still in tip top shape for his age.

I looked to my left and Coach Smooth was standing in the doorway. "Good morning sir, Mr. Martin isn't it?" They shook hands, but you could tell Mr. Martin didn't really respect Coach Smooth.

"Yes, I'm trying to figure out why my students aren't in class."

"One of their teammates was killed la-"

"I know about Buddy's death. Regardless, they should be in class."

Coach Smooth took a deep breath, then said "Mrs. Dixon told them they could gather at my office to be together."

"Why does she think that'll help anything?

"Well…the situation might be overwhelming for them. Being together helps them grieve."

Mr. Martin started laughing and looked at me, shaking his head. "You remember what happened last month Mr. Martin, when Denise got killed. We couldn't barely learn nothing 'cause people was crying so much" I pleaded. He didn't look convinced. "You kids man" he said, still laughing. "I swear the older I get, the less I understand y'all." I put my head down and stared at the floor.

"Well maybe that's because you don't understand what they're dealing with." Everybody turned and looked at Coach Smooth. We were shocked. All these years, we had never heard nobody talk to Mr. Martin like that. Not even Principal Dixon!

"Ohh I've met their parents. I know what they're dealing with at home. Children raising children."

"Yes, their elders have failed them. But not just their biological ones, we all fail them by not being empathetic enough."

Mr. Martin straightened up and smiled. He looked like he was sizing Coach Smooth up. Mr. Martin was about a foot taller than Coach Smooth, so he looked down on him both literally and figuratively. "Where did you go to college young man?" he asked. Coach Smooth was 40 years old, how the hell was he a young man?

"I didn't go to college sir" Coach Smooth said.

"Ah, why not? If you don't mind me asking." Coach Smooth swallowed his spit, which was really him swallowing his pride, and said "Because I went to prison when I was 17." Everybody on the floor looked at each other. We could tell Coach Smooth had gone through a lot in his life, but he never talked about it, and we didn't ask. He had a bullet wound on his left forearm, and he always got respect from the people at the other schools we played against. They treated him like a legend. I didn't like what Mr. Martin was doing; it was like watching someone try to embarrass your father.

"I honestly wish that had been Buddy's fate as well. God bless his soul" Mr. Martin said. "Well I wouldn't wish prison on any one. Many nights I wished I was dead inside that cell." Mr. Martin frowned. "That's very extreme. And I don't believe those kinds of views should be shared in front of kids." You could tell by the look on Coach's face that he was tired of Mr. Martin. I think his patience had run out.

"But I've always been an advocate of our young men joining the military once out of high school. You all should seriously consider that" Mr. Martin said.

"What will that solve? They already grew up in war zones, what will going to another war zone and fighting Arabs do exactly?"

"The military gives kids discipline. And character."

"We can give them that right HERE. Only thing gon' come from the military is brainwashing. That's all them white folk gon' do to 'em."

"Ohh, I see. You're one of those" Mr. Martin said, smiling again.

"One of what?"

"One of those people who blame everything on the white man." Coach Smooth rolled his eyes, but said nothing. "Well I've got news for you: All of our woes can't be blamed on them. These kids aren't killing each other because of white people. It's the music they listen to. That damn Rap B.S. How can they call that music? I've always hated it. And have you heard the slang they use? It sounds like they're creating their own words."

"You know how the English language was created?" Coach Smooth asked.

"How is that?"

"They made it up!"

Everybody on the floor laughed, but Mr. Martin didn't seem amused.

"Well regardless, the white man isn't the one waiting for you in the alley with a gun."

"The white man MADE the gun fool!"

Everybody laughed again. This was our first time seeing someone get the best of Mr. Martin, and we weren't afraid to laugh in his face. You could tell he didn't like losing arguments. Boy, I wish Buddy was here to see this. "You watch who you're calling a fool. I'm old enough to remember having to ride at the back of the streetcar. I think I know a thing or two about racism." He always brought that up to make us feel bad. I swear, he act like we was the ones hit his ass with a water hose back then.

"I meant no disrespect sir, I apologize" Coach Smooth said. Mr. Martin shook his head, looked around at us on the floor, then turned and walked away. "I'll be speaking with Mrs. Dixon shortly" he said. The bell rang, it was time for second period now. Coach Smooth walked back into his office. No one on the floor moved. Buddy was dead...

BOURBON STREET BAPTISM

We walked into the convenience store and there was a long ass line. Since it was Mardi Gras, any other place we went would be just as packed, so I wasn't leaving. And Brothers Food Mart was the cheapest place to buy liquor around Canal Street. The French Quarter be having them high ass prices, straight finessing them tourists out their money.

As I made my way through the store, I noticed a Trans-woman staring at me from the checkout line, smiling hard as hell. I took a deep breath and kept walking. "Ohh my gawd" the Trans-woman said, in a thick country accent. Everybody in the store started giggling. Then Ziggy, who was walking behind me the whole time, said "Ain't no oh my gawd, I'll beat the fuck out you up in here." I kept walking, but Ziggy stopped, looking like he was ready to swing. You could tell the Trans-woman was probably from Atlanta or something, in town for Mardi Gras. I guess they get down a lil' different out there. "We don't play that shit down here. Nigga will buss yo' fuckin' head open" Ziggy said. A man who was also standing in line, wearing a kitchen apron, chuckled and said "Real shit."

At this point I was in the back of the store, standing in the juice aisle, acting like I wasn't even with Ziggy 'cause I ain't want to get put out the store. The Trans-woman kept looking forward, and never said another word. Ziggy finally caught up with me and said "They be trippin' son. Same shit happened the other night. A car pull up and the driver say 'Wassup with y'all.' I knew something wasn't right brudda, 'cause since when a car full of girls gonna pull up on two random dudes, late at night, trying to flirt? I said 'Wusham' though, you know, trying not to seem spooked. We mixing the D'ussé with lemonade, right?"

"Yea" I said.

"So boom, the driver told me 'Come here'. Whole time I'm expecting a nigga to hop out the backseat with a big ass .40, and rob my stupid ass. But I walked to the car anyway. I could see somebody was in the passenger seat, and two people in the backseat. The driver said 'What y'all trying to do?' I swear, I knew something wasn't right Zo." We were in line now, and I was listening intently to his story. Ziggy was one of them people who made you wanna listen when he talked, even if he got carried away sometimes. "Greg was behind me, and he flashed the light from his phone in the car. I heard him say 'Man that's niggas'. Bitch my heart dropped to my ass. Everybody in the car had on wigs and make-up. They hit the gas so quick and sped off. I wish I had my burner, I would've lit that car up with holes."

We put our stuff on the counter, and I pointed to the bottle of D'ussé on the shelf for the man behind the register to get. Only $35, I knew it. Guaranteed, in the French Quarter they charging like $50.

"You owe me seven cents" the clerk said. Ziggy twisted his face up and said "Man bye, you better let us go with seven cents. You Black or Arab?" Another clerk, who was sweeping in the aisle behind us, said "He's Ethiopian." Ziggy turned back to the man behind the register and shouted "MAN THAT'S BLACK!" All the clerks laughed. Ziggy smiled, said "You better start acting like it", and walked out of the store. I gave the clerk a dime and told him to keep the change.

We walked toward Canal street, squeezing our way around drunk tourists and children on candy highs. Me and Ziggy both had on Timb' boots, he had on butters, I had on black ones though.

Ziggy had a soulja rag tied around his dreadlocks. I had a fresh cut, so I was feeling myself. A brass band was playing a block off Bourbon street, so we posted up across the street to listen. About 20 yards away, a white woman raised up her shirt and her titties popped out. Then a string of beads longer than her arm fell from the balcony above and thwacked her in the face. Ziggy laughed and opened the D'ussé bottle. We had a pretty good spot on Bourbon street. People weren't bumping into us, we were listening to some good live music, and we could see every beautiful woman who walked up the street.

We finished our first cup and I was feeling good. Out of my peripheral, I could see two people walking toward us. It was an Asian dude and a Middle Eastern-looking girl. They looked like they weren't even 21 yet. "Hey guys, how's it going?" We ain't say shit, we just looked at them. "Okay, just enjoying the scenes aye?" We still ain't say nothing, just sipped our drinks. "Well, my name's Tim, and this is Aesha, can we share some great news with you about our lord and savior Jesus Christ?"

Great. We ain't even been out here ten minutes and gotta get preached too. And of course, out of all the drunk white people on Bourbon street, it's US who look like we need some saving. Two niggas.

I noticed that they came at us the same way the military would when they did recruits at our high school. One time this white man in all camo tried to talk to me after school, but I kept walking on him. Didn't wanna waste his time. Few minutes later, Mack told me that the military dude was walking around the school, bad-mouthing me. He told people that I was gon' be a failure in life because I wouldn't stop and talk to him. Shit kind of hurt my feelings, but that's the mind games they try to play with people.

"We won't take much of your time. I promise. Do you go to church?" Tim broke my train of thought.

"Yes" I said.

"How often?"

"Every sunday."

He look surprised. "Well that's good to hear, I'd like to give you this." Tim handed me a pamphlet with a big ass white Jesus on it. Ziggy bussed out laughing. I noticed Aesha, who hadn't said a word so far, looked very nervous.

"You got something for me?" Ziggy asked Aesha. She jumped, like she didn't expect to be acknowledged. "Oh, no" she said, and laughed nervously. For some reason, Tim was ignoring Ziggy and directing his questions towards me. A lady wearing a hair net stopped in front of us and asked if we had a lighter. Ziggy handed her his, and she pulled out a pack of cigarettes. She looked like she had just gotten off of work and was on her way home.

"Y'all not from here huh?" Ziggy asked Aesha.

"No, we're from Virginia."

"But your parents weren't born in this country?"

They seemed shocked by the question, and didn't answer.

"See, me and my potna Zo, our people been in this country for a long time" Ziggy said, glancing at me. "And we got a strange relationship with that book in your hands." He pointed at the bible Tim carried. "That book ain't caused nothing but problems for us."

Tim looked stumped, like he didn't expect us to give him this much trouble. He looked at Aesha for help. "Do you believe in God?" she quickly asked.

"I believe they got some kind of meaning behind all this shit we going through. And I went to church last Sunday. Thanks for asking" Ziggy said.

"Sounds like you've lost your faith."

"Well, faith is a language. I ain't speaking faith right now. I'm speaking reality." At that moment, I noticed the lady in the hairnet had never left. She was listening to our conversation, smoking her cigarette. "The bible the reason why our people be on some turn the other cheek type stuff when dealing with these racists out here. I swear, sometimes I hate old people 'cause they let them white folk do that sick shit to them back in the day."

"They didn't LET them do it, but..." the lady in the hairnet retorted. She looked like she was about 54 or 55. Not quite old, but old enough to feel like she had to speak up.

"SEE, see? That right there. They didn't let them do it, BUT…" said Ziggy.

"You ain't supposed to hate people. God gon' strike you down for that." She was scornfully looking at Ziggy, like a mother though.

"The Bible should've been taken away from them mothafuckas back in the G. Shit would be WAY better today."

"Boy what the Bible got to do with corrupt-minded ass white people?"

Tim and Aesha listened to this exchange, visibly alarmed.

"White people, they don't use all that God and Jesus talk" Ziggy said.

"Yea some of them do."

"SOME of them do, but ALL niggas do."

"Yes and I'm one of 'em. I believe in Jesus, and you do too. You better." The lady nodded her head at us, like a mother. "Yea ya' right" Ziggy said, smirking. "I'ma see y'all around" she said, waved, and walked away.

About five seconds of silence went by as all four of us watched the lady leave. Four Black boys were beating on buckets with drumsticks at the end of the block. A crowd of people had gathered around them. I decided to break the silence.

"How old are y'all?"

"20" Tim said. Aesha said "19" and looked down, awkwardly. "Y'all missionaries or something?" Ziggy asked. They both shook their heads in affirmation.

"We the first people y'all talked to today?"

"No, we've talked to a few people before you. I don't know how much longer we'll be out here though."

"Well good luck with it" I told them.

"Yea good luck. They got a lot of people to talk to out here" Ziggy said, and shook their hands. Tim had an enlightened look on his face, as if he learned something from us. Aesha waved as they walked away. I chucked up the deuce at 'em.

I looked at Ziggy and sighed. He started patting his pockets.

"Bruh."

"What?"
"That lady took my fucking lighter."

INVITED TO THE COOKOUT

I was on the grill, sipping E&J. We always bought a bottle of E&J because it was only $12, and got you drunk pretty fast. Other than that, we drank daiquiris because they were even cheaper. That's the college life: getting drunk on a budget. We had some fees pulling up later, hopefully I could take a shower before then. Can't be smelling like chicken around the girls.

Jaron brought me another cup of E&J before I could even finish my first. At this rate, I would be drunk before the food was even done.

"Say dawg, is you gon' cook something too? All you doing is drinking" I said.

Jaron laughed at me and turned on the stereo. We stayed up late the night before adding music to our playlist. It was the perfect amalgamation of cookout classics, old school joints, and ass shaking music. Over 1000 songs, we knew to save the ass shaking selection for later when the fees pulled up. Now we was vibin' to everything from Big Tymers to Cameo.

Most of the food was done by 3 P.M., and the rest of our friends had arrived. I was slurred at this point, and still hadn't eaten. Me, Nardy, and Jaron was on the porch. Everybody else was inside playing 2K. That's when a Grey Honda pulled into the driveway. None of us recognized the car, so we stood up. Ro got out the passenger side with a daiquiri in his hand. "Y'all ready to cut up?" he asked. A Shia LaBeouf looking ass white boy got out from the driver's side. "Aye y'all, this is my coworker Russ. I told him he could come, long as he brought a gallon of daiquiri for us." We dapped Russell off, and exchanged pleasantries and shit.

"Go make Russell a plate" I told Ro.

"Nah, he gon make his own damn plate."

They went inside and came back out with their food. "Hey this chicken is pretty good Pat" Russ said to me. "Appreciate it bruh. The burgers are almost done."

After I finished cooking, we sat out there talking and eating for another half hour. Just smoking, sipping, knowing we all had to go to class in the morning. Enjoying our day off. Anita Baker was playing on the stereo, perfect smoking music. The fees was gonna pull up in about 2 hours. The day was going perfect, and Russ seemed like a cool ass white boy. I was glad Ro invited him to the cookout.

Nardy stood up and said "Man we gotta get right before the fees come over here." Everybody looked around at each other. "Fuck it. Shots?" I asked. Everybody grunted, but they knew they couldn't back down.

After three shots, Russ stood up and exclaimed "Alright let's get this party started nigga! Change the music, the fuck are y'all listening to?" Ro and Jaron laughed; me and Nardy didn't. We just shot each other a glance. Russ went inside, turned off the Anita Baker we was playing, and put on fucking Post Malone. I couldn't believe this shit. I just stared at the ground in disbelief. The fact that he switched into a whole 'nother person so abruptly made it surreal. I stood up, poured the rest of my drink in the grass, and walked toward the door. Russ was walking out at the same time. He put his hand up to high five me. I looked him in his eyes and kept walking. I overheard him say "The fuck is his problem?" before the door closed.

I went to the living room and sat on the couch. Gary and Lou were in there playing 2K. "What's up Pat baby" Lou said and dapped me off. I sat next to them, blowed, and agitated. I wasn't even drunk no more. That's how annoyed I was. The alcohol in my body got cancelled out. Make it worst, that new Eminem album where he was rapping on all the Trap beats was playing on the stereo. "Son, turn that stupid ass shit off" Gary said. I ain't get up, and they couldn't hear him on the porch.

He said "nigga", changed our music, and they laughed…

I really couldn't wrap my head around it. That's one of the main reasons why I ain't a fan of inviting outsiders to our cookouts. But if one of us puts in money for food, then we can invite who the fuck we want. Thems the rules…

After five more minutes of Eminem rhyming "fucking zebra" with Justin Bieber, and "Islamic regime" with washing machine, I guess Gary had enough.

"Son that shit throwing me off. I ain't scored a point since that been playing" he said. He put the game on pause, got up from his chair and unplugged the stereo.

Five minutes later, white boy came inside and asked "Yo what happened to the music?" Everybody shrugged. He walked into the bathroom, so I went back on the porch and asked "What's up with that dude bruh?" Ro laughed and Jaron looked confused. Nardy just smirked. "What happened?" Jaron asked. "He said nigga, then he changed the music. He seem cool but that kind of rubbed me wrong." Jaron took a swig of his drink and said "Man it's the 21st Century. I feel like white people should be able to say nigga!" Everybody just looked at his stupid ass. Even the squirrel climbing up the tree stopped what he was doing and looked at that nigga.

"He don't act like this at work. I think it's the liquor" Ro said. "Drunk mind speak what?" I asked. "Sober mothafuckin' thoughts" Ro said, and shook his head.

White boy came back on the porch and said "When are the hoes getting here?" Everybody except me and Nardy laughed. For the rest of the evening Russ and Jaron were best friends. I took a long shower to get that BBQ smell off of me, and I started to feel better. While in the bathroom I heard ass shaking music playing on the stereo, that meant the girls were here. I heard female voices in the hallway, and everybody sounded happy to see each other.

I dried off and sat on my bed wearing nothing but a towel. Somebody knocked on my door and opened it before I could answer. It was April. "Pat in here? Ohh" she said, seeing that I wasn't dressed. I laughed and said "No damn manners."

"Ohh my God, I'm so sorry" she said. Russ walked in the room and screamed "Y'all about to get freaky?" Bitch we might have been but you just blew it. April laughed and said "No I was just leaving", then walked out of the room. Now I was sitting on the bed, in my towel, looking at Russell. "Don't keep the hoes waiting" he said, and walked out of the room.

I put on some clothes and walked into the living room about ten minutes later. The girls, all seven of them, were twerking on Russ, while Jaron recorded it on his phone. If you ever seen one of them videos of women dancing on cops at carnival, that's what they looked like. Russ kept lifting their shorts and skirts up, all you saw was cheeks and thongs, and every time the girls did nothing but laugh and put his hand down. I would've got smacked for doing that.

I walked straight to the kitchen to make a drink and saw Nardy in there.

"Beer pong?"

"You ain't on my level. C'mon!"

We cleared the table off and started playing. Me and Dejanae beat Nardy and April the first game. Next, we beat Gary and Darionne. Then, Lou and Tori. We were on a roll!

Then we played against Russ and Jaron. As Russ got more drunk, he said nigga three more times, and called Dejanae a hoe, to which she simply laughed. "Aye chill out with that" I told him. "Aww c'mon man, she's doesn't mind" he said. I couldn't figure out why everybody was letting him get away with so much. I done seen these muh'fuckas act paranoid when a Black dude we don't know walks on the porch, and it ends up being the pizza man. But let one white boy come around and everybody acts an ass.

We all played beer pong for another hour, then sat down to play truth or dare.

Right off the bat, Russ looked at Darionne and said "I dare you to suck my big toe for $200. You know you need it." He finally crossed the line, I thought. I waited for Darionne to tell him off. Then she said "Pull the money out!" I couldn't believe it. Jaron got some whipped cream from the kitchen and handed it to Russ, who sprayed some onto his foot. The rest of the girls didn't look happy.

Tori said "C'mon Darionne, you had too much to drink." Darionne pushed her away. "Bitch let me go, I'm gon' make this $200."

"Pat can I take her to your room?" April asked.

"Yea go ahead. Let her lay down." Russ pushed the girls back and said "Nope, she's not going anywhere." Darionne dropped down to her knees and put the whole toe in her mouth. Jaron screamed, live streaming it on his social media. "Don't record this shit bruh" Tori said. Ro got up from the couch and tried to take control of the situation, seeing as how Russ was his guest. "Alright bruh. You doing too much now" he said. "No she's not done. Darionne you missed a spot sweetie." Nardy grabbed Darionne and said "Nah she's done." The whole room got quiet now. Russ didn't challenge Nardy, which was a smart decision. Unlike me, he really would've put hands on Russ. Darionne grabbed the $200 of the table, and Nardy guided her to his room so she could lay down.

"That shit was lit" Russ said. Tori went to check on Darionne, and the rest of the girls looked at Russ in disgust. He didn't care though. He just went into the bathroom to wash off his foot, laughing as he bumped into multiple chairs own his way there.

Five minutes later he came back into the living room holding a to-go plate.

"Aye man, it was nice hanging with y'all, but I gotta go."

"You sure you're not too fucked up to drive dude?" Ro asked him.

"Hell no man, I'm good. I do this all the time." He dapped Ro and Jaron off and walked over to where I was sitting. I waved his hand out of my face. "I'm good" I said. He looked at Ro, and Ro shrugged. After he left, me, Gary, and Lou went to check on Darionne. Jaron and Ro went into the kitchen. I heard Jaron scream "That mothafucka ate all the chicken!"

DNA TESTS: THE NEWEST THREAT TO BLACK IDENTITY (ANCESTRYDNA, 23ANDME)

African Americans have a fragile identity.

During slavery, we lost all knowledge of who we were before being enslaved. Mentally, we went from being the oldest people on Earth, to the youngest (African history is at least 200,000 years old; while African American history is only 500). When your inception as a people begins with you in chains, it greatly affects how you see yourself.

On a wider scale, African descendants exist all around the world due to both forced and voluntary migrations. We all make up the African Diaspora. Concurrently, non-Black historians and anthropologists have been imposing their opinions and assessments on OUR history, while having complete autonomy over THEIRS. Every time we've tried to reconnect with Africa, and embrace our Blackness, non-Blacks have tainted with our movements. Marcus Garvey, who founded a ship line to bring Blacks in the Americas back to West Africa, was stalked by J. Edgar Hoover (who would go on to run the FBI) and deported out of the country. They infiltrate and co-opt our organizations, then promote certain Black people who push agendas that they approve of. After years of seeing starving children in Africa on commercials, accompanied with whites asking for one dollar a day, we are now ashamed of our origins. In school, we learn nothing about Africa, but know all about Europe. Blacks with white minds; all of us.

So we distance ourselves from that land. Even our supposed intellectuals do this, some wishing to be called "Black American" instead of African American. The emergence of companies like *23andMe* and *Ancestry.Com Inc* have led to an interest in discovering more about our family history through DNA testing. These tests affect African Americans differently than they do others. People with fragile identities, knowing more about Europe than they do about Africa, who look at a DNA test and see "12% Irish"? Danger lurks...

Most of us either wish to transcend our Blackness, or are self-conscious about our Blackness. We see European "ancestry" and either smile in delight, or feel we aren't Black enough. I put "ancestry" in quotations because a man who raped and held my family member captive is not my ancestor, nor should he be seen as yours.

Our feelings of inferiority leads to us being more inclusive of other groups than those groups are to us. For example, when the National Museum of African American History and Culture opened in 2016, *Loving* was chosen for its first film screening. *Loving* is the story of a couple who were the plaintiffs in a 1967 U.S. Supreme Court decision which invalidated state laws prohibiting interracial marriage. The plaintiffs were Robert Loving, a white American male, and Mildred Loving, a woman who denied having any African ancestry, and instead attested to being Native American.[1] Rhea L. Combs, the museum's film curator, said "Showing the film ... is important because the story is symbolic of the mission of the museum. It demonstrates the link between people of all backgrounds and cultures."[2] So the first film shown at a museum about African American history was (1) technically not about African Americans, since Mildred didn't identify as Black, and (2) also about White Americans. But due to Comb's statement about the museum's mission, it seems they did exactly what they were aiming for.

So why are we so inclusive of other groups, even in spaces that were created to focus on us? For clarity, let's examine the history of our struggle for identity, and overall survival, when imposed upon by outside groups who've literally tried to wipe us off of the planet.

The African Diaspora is considered as the forced migration of Africans during the Arab Slave Trade (7th century-20th century), and of West, Central, and East Africans during the European Slave Trade (15th century-19th century). These forced migrations led to African communities existing everywhere from Pakistan to Saint Lucia! Additionally, African descendants exist on a cluster of islands in the Pacific and Indian Oceans, due to an assumed voluntary migration out of Africa thousands of years ago. In the 16th century, when Spanish missionaries were operating in the Philippines, the term "Negrito" (or little Black person) was coined for the indigenous people they observed on the island. In 1756, Charles De Brosses theorized that there was an "old black race" of the Pacific, who he believed were conquered by the peoples of what is now known as Polynesia. He distinguished the conquerors as having "lighter skin". When observing the Aeta peoples , Spanish explorers described them as "fearsome warriors". However, their lack of organization and small numbers made them vulnerable to outsiders. Other groups seeking slaves would take advantage of the Aetas' internal feuding (sound familiar?), capture them, and sell them into slavery.

In Australia, white settlers developed plans for "breeding out" the Aborigines, with people like Dr. Cecil Cook (Chief Protector of Aborigines and noted white Supremacist) stating as follows: *"...generally by the fifth and invariably by the sixth generation, all native characteristics of the Australian Aborigine are eradicated. The problem of our half-castes will quickly be eliminated by the complete disappearance of the [B]lack race, and the swift submergence of their progeny in the white."*[3]

As it is in America, cultural (and biological) assimilation became the way of the land in Australia. A.O. Neville (also Chief "Protector" of Aborigines) said: *"Eliminate the full-blood and per-*

mit the white admixture to half-castes and eventually the race will become white."[4]

But now, after years of describing these native folk as Black, Europeans seem to have changed their minds. Indigenous folk of the Philippines, for example, are described by some white Anthropologists as "Proto-Australoid", "Paleo-Mediterranean", and not direct descendants of Africa. Interestingly (and conveniently timed), this new description comes after a recent period of Aboriginal activists embracing the term "Black" and using their ancestry as a source of pride.

On the subject of Ancient Kemet (Egypt), white authors describe the word Kemet as meaning "Black", in reference to the black soil of the area. Some African historians refute this, saying Kemet refers to the indigenous people of the land, who were Black. The popular theme in all these cases, is that the arguments most accepted are those by the white authors, anthropologists, etc. They are viewed as credible sources on African/Black history, while the claims of actual Africans/Blacks are dismissed as irredentism.

So how did this phenomenon come about of those who are not Black or African determining who is and who isn't? And why are Europeans so obsessed with how we view ourselves? This continues today, for example, with CNN producing documentaries like the aptly titled "Who is Black in America?"[5], further perpetuating confusion among an already confused and insecure group of people. Something many Blacks in America have in common with Mildred Loving, is that they also attest to having Indian ancestors. If someone in our family has less "nappy" hair, we attribute it to a Native American or Creole family member whom none of us have ever met. This is something I call the "Exotic Negro Complex". We subconsciously want to transcend being Black, or be Black AND (...). Anything other than that, is just regular, boring, Blackness.

DNA tests (genetic admixture tests, more specifically) are reliable only a few hundred years back. After all, if all humans come from Africa, surely whites would have African blood (according to this theory). So how do DNA tests break down 200,000 years of ancestry into a 100% scale? The answer is, they don't. You have thousands (probably millions) of ancestors, and when you have a child, they inherit your partner's ancestry, too. Modern science hasn't developed yet to the point where they can trace your full ancestry. Yet the companies offering DNA tests can't educate you on this (too much at least), because after all, it is a business, and this would make consumers more skeptical.

Jamilah Lemieux, Senior Editor for Ebony Magazine, was the subject of an article written by William Bryant Miles pertaining to a DNA test she took with *23andMe*.[6] Her DNA results from this company alleged that she had more European "ancestry" than African. In the article written about Lemieux's DNA results are examples of the confusion, passivity, and identity complexes that exist among African Americans. For example, Miles describes how he prefers the term "Black American, which inherently includes African Ancestry, but is rooted in a truly American identity."[6] He continues, stating "Black American pays homage to Harriet Tubman, Frederick Douglass, the slaves, who I think are descendants of, but distinct from, continental Africans. I view Africa as my grandmother, America as my mother, albeit she is an abusive one…"[6] This is a very descriptive, yet passive characterization. Miles double distances himself from Africa. He views himself not only as "distinct from continental Africans", but not even as an African American. And as we've learned, America has fought hard for us to be this submissive. In other words, his choice of identity accepts defeat.

Miles goes on to describe himself as a "regular, schmegular Black boy."[6] Note the term "regular". He's "regular" Black, unlike the exotic and fancy Black exhibited in Ms. Lemieux's DNA results. When Miles receives his own results, and he sees "European: 22.9%", he claims "Essentially, one fourth of my ancestry is not Black. That's basically a grandparent."[6] This is yet another example of our submissiveness. He refers to the white men who held his family members captive against their will (and impregnated several of them, most likely through rape) as his ancestors/

grandparents. Words are important. This is why using the term "family member" resonates with us more than "ancestor". "Family member" gives us a sense of closeness and urgency. It's more personal, while "ancestor" gives distance. Furthermore, calling a slave owner what he is: a slave owner, is an absolute truth. Calling them your ancestor humanizes them, and puts them on an equal level with your real ancestors, whose lives they made a living hell. If someone raped and impregnated your grandmother, you wouldn't claim his blood; you would rebuke it. And you surely wouldn't call him your grandfather, you would call him what he is: a rapist.

Yet other Black writers share Miles' sentiments,[7] feeling disconnected (and sometimes pushed away) from Africa and its people, ultimately leading to them accepting this disconnect. But here's the thing: these are writers for popular websites and magazines that have the power to influence some very impressionable Black people. If this was done purposely, I would call it propaganda. But I don't think any of our young Black brothers and sisters mean malice. So in this case, it is irresponsibility.

African Americans often exaggerate our differences with continental Africans, overlooking the similarities. Just the fact that we still share a lot in common culturally tells us something about how deep our roots are, especially after the attempts made by others to destroy them. But no matter how light skinned you are, or how straight your hair is, there is someone on the African continent who looks exactly like you. This is something that modern science cannot explain. It's what makes an Afro-Mexican girl resemble an Aeta; or a Creole girl in New Orleans resemble an Eritrean or Khoisan girl. No matter what you do to us, where you force us to migrate to, and how you taint with our DNA, we still resemble one another. A very divine gift. One that is not cause for passive distinction; but for aggressive solidarity.

BLACK MUSIC AND OUR RELUCTANCE TO CLAIM IT

In the French Quarter of New Orleans, a Jazz band is busking. The band is all white, and sounds very good. A 30-something year old Black woman walks past the band, holding hands with her son. At that same moment, a "wigger" looking white guy with neck tattoos drives around the corner, blasting Lil Wayne from his stereo, drowning out the band. The Black woman starts to dance and yells toward the car, "That's right, play OUR music".

The fact that this woman didn't know Jazz music was created by Black people didn't shock me, because at one point in my life I probably didn't know either. Not knowing is one thing, but being arrogant while not knowing is another. Once arrogance is involved, it goes from ignorance to stupidity.

But is Jazz Black music? When the genre first came into the spotlight about 100 years ago, many whites called it jungle music, or simply, noise. But as time went on, and Jazz gained recognition worldwide, whites exaggerated their input, often out right claiming that Blacks stole the music from them. Coincidentally, there has been a similar debate in the Hip Hop community. Some say Hip Hop is indeed Black culture, but since it has been embraced across the globe, all races are welcome to participate. Yet others say that although the majority of Rap pioneers were Black, there were individual white people who were instrumental in the success of Black rappers, thus making the creation a colorless, multicultural thing. What's the difference between the two debates? Our elders weren't as confused as us when they created Jazz. Back then, a white person could aid you to success, and still call you the "N word". Since then, things have changed…a little. One of the worse things a white person can do to a Black person is be nice to them. It confuses the hell out of us, especially when our understanding of racism is on an elementary level. It'll have us challenging a victim of racism, and defending a person who exploits us, all the while thinking we are doing the right thing.

In 1915, while touring the Vaudeville circuit, New Orleans native Freddie Keppard was offered an opportunity to make what would've been the first ever jazz recording. For reasons still disputed, he declined the offer from the Victor Recording Company. Two years later, the Original Dixieland Jazz Band traveled to New York and recorded two sides for Victor, both of which took the nation by storm. Freddie Keppard was Black; the Original Dixieland Jazz Band was white.

To attract attention, the band was promoted as the "Creators of Jazz". Nick LaRocca, leader of ODJB, was quoted as saying: *"Our music is strictly white man's music…My contention is that the Negroes learned to play this rhythm and music from the whites…The Negro did not play any kind of music equal to white men at any time."*[1]

We'll get back to that *rhythm* LaRocca spoke of, but to be liberal, ODJB did in fact have a major impact on early Jazz. The band helped spread the genre to households across the country. But be clear, they weren't the creators. In fact, the genres that laid the blueprint for what would become Jazz had already existed for decades; some of them, since slavery.

Art Blakey, famed Jazz drummer and bandleader, was once quoted as saying: *"No America, no jazz. I've seen people try to connect it to other countries, for instance to Africa, but it doesn't have a damn thing to do with Africa."*[2]

He was right about the America part. Jazz wouldn't exist if it weren't for Blacks being enslaved and forced upon these shores. But to say Africa had nothing to do with the creation of Jazz is horribly inaccurate. See, wherever Europeans went on this planet, they practiced a form of white supremacy unique to the land they were invading. For example, in the early 1900s while white America was rallying against miscegenation, their cousins were colonizing Australia and using miscegenation as a tool to "breed out" the Black Aboriginal population. So while it was common practice in North America for slave masters to strip away the culture of those they held in bondage, in South America and the Caribbean things were a bit different. Go to places like Cuba, Brazil, or Haiti and you'll see descendants of slaves performing dances and even speaking languages native to Africa. But there was one particular place in the United States where Africans were allowed to maintain some aspects of their culture: Louisiana (New Orleans has actually been called the "northernmost part of the Caribbean" by some).

Congo square was the place where the enslaved, Creoles of Color, and free Black community all congregated on Sundays. They'd dance, sing, trade, and socialize. Observers recounted the various dances performed like Bamboula, Calinda, Congo, Carabine, and Juba. Louis Gottschalk, a man whose race remains unclear, was the first American pianist (of any race) whose works gained international exposure. His compositions like "Bamboula" (1848) foreshadowed Ragtime and Jazz, genres that would not exist until many years later. Many of his works were inspired by the dances and *rhythms* he heard at Congo Square as a child. Gottschalk was a prodigy at age 11, making his debut at the St. Charles Hotel. Two years later, at age 13, Gottschalk was performing at concerts in France, at one point receiving applause from Frédéric Chopin himself. Next, he traveled to Latin America and parts of the Caribbean, soaking in even more sounds of the Black diaspora. It's possible that Gottschalk came across the predecessor of what would become "Salsa" music while in Cuba, a component Jelly Roll Morton called the "Spanish Tinge". Morton said this element was essential to playing Jazz correctly (fun fact:

there once was a ferry that ran from New Orleans to Havana!)

In the early days of Reconstruction, New Orleans had a very large Italian population. This was a peculiar moment in the city's history, and the newly arrived immigrants struggled to adapt. But even after participating in local politics, and showing their allegiance to the Democratic Party, they still faced discrimination from other European groups. It was Sicilians verses Maltese, and Spaniards verses Greeks, while the American born whites looked down on them all. Some Italians were members of white supremacist groups like the Innocenti, stalking polls on election day to keep Blacks from voting, and marching through the French Quarter while armed as an intimidation technique. All this reached its climax in 1890, when the city's chief of police was assassinated. Blame was quickly placed on an obscure Italian organization called the Mafia (New Orleans has been acknowledged by many as the birthplace of the American Mob). Dozens of people were arrested with no evidence of their involvement. 19 men were eventually indicted, but this resulted in nothing but mistrials and acquittals. On March 14th, 1891, a white mob frustrated with the trial's outcome formed outside the prison, and 11 of the men were dragged from their jail cells and lynched. The Italian community's attempts at assimilation and white acceptance had a very rocky start.

Danny Barker was an important figure in New Orleans Jazz history. He outlived most of his contemporaries, and was able to publish multiple books and give countless interviews in his lifetime. In one of these interviews, he gave his two cents on La-Rocca's claim that Blacks stole Jazz from whites. He said: *"It was a great pattern in New Orleans for parade bands to stop at the corner of (Italian) grocery stores…to get refreshments. So the Italian boys had a good idea of what the negroes were playing. A whole lot of them did not play this Jazz music because they could always make a living playing legitimate music. Theatres, and concerts, and Operas, and everything else."*[3]

Months before ODJB made the first commercial Jazz recordings, Variety Magazine addressed a wide spread debate over the origins of Jazz. There was a misconception that the music originated in Chicago, since many Louisiana jazzmen and women moved there during the Great Migration. Variety went on record acknowledging New Orleans as its birthplace. Furthermore, the article came at the perfect time, because it conflicts with LaRocca's future statements about Jazz's racial origins. In its November 1916 edition, the magazine wrote: *"Chicago's claim to originating 'Jazz Bands' and 'Balling the Jack' are as groundless, according to Variety's New Orleans correspondent, as Frisco's assuming to be the locale for the first 'Todolo' and 'Turkey Trot' dances. Little negro tots were 'Ballin' the Jack' in New Orleans over ten years ago, and negro roustabouts were 'Turkey Trotting' and doing the 'Todolo' in New Orleans as far back as 1890, he says. 'Jazz Bands' have been popular there for over two years, and Chicago cabaret owners brought entertainers from that city to introduce the idea."*[4]

Nevertheless, by the early 1920s, the Jazz musicians most popular in the country were white men. Upon hearing the music for the first time, Paul Whiteman (a very fitting last name) was set on, in his words, "making a lady" out of Jazz. The media publicized Whiteman as the "King of Jazz", disregarding King Bolden, King Keppard, and especially King Oliver, who had the Chicago night scene on fire at the time. One of Whiteman's trumpet players, a teenager by the name of Bix Beiderbecke, often snuck out of his suburban home in Davenport, Iowa, to hear what he called "real jazz niggers" on the Southside of Chicago. In regards to this, Barker said: *"Paul Whiteman was the King of Jazz and...I never known him to play a Jazz note. That's America's publicity...20 or 30 years later, Benny Goodman comes up, and he'll tell you all the time he used to go listen to Johnny Dodds play. And they named him the King of Swing...it's a very 'ticular situation. But I noticed, Nick LaRocca, he played a Jazz which is not the same as King Oliver's Jazz. It was diluted of something...If you notice, the Dixieland records, they're all speeded up. They have a tendency to burlesque the music...Rarely would (a white band) play a series of low down blues tunes...They don't have the blues like a negro has because he's never been oppressed like that...They say they created (Jazz)? They created THEIR style."*[3]

In the years following WWII, Rhythm & Blues surpassed Jazz as the most popular genre. This was made possible by a split in the Jazz community over a new style of playing called "Bebop" that most older Jazz musicians couldn't stand. By the late 1950s, Rock 'n Roll was the craze of the nation, and toward the end of the tragic decade of the 1960s, Soul music and Motown were the voice of the youth. As time went on, and Blacks created new forms of music, people like Elvis Presley, The Beatles, and The Rolling Stones constantly emerged as the face of these respective genres. The story usually went as follows: Young white guys discovered music of some underappreciated Black artist, they fell in love with it, studied it, learned to play it, and eventually became more popular than the artist who inspired them. In 1973, Margo Jefferson published a piece on this topic in Harper's magazine. She wrote: *"The night Jimi (Hendrix) died I dreamed this was the latest step in a plot being designed to eliminate [B]lacks from rock music so that it may be recorded in history as a creation of whites. Future generations, my dream ran, will be taught that while rock may have had its beginnings among [B]lacks, it had its true flowering among whites. The best [B]lack artists will thus be studied as remarkable primitives who unconsciously foreshadowed future developments."*[5]

So back to our initial story: why didn't the lady in the French Quarter know that Black people created Jazz? It's mostly because we moved on from the genre decades before she was even born. The only place in America that you can see an all-Black band play traditional Jazz is in New Orleans. Go to New York or Chicago, and the only Jazz you'll hear Black musicians play is Bebop. Many of them grew up on people like Miles Davis, or Coltrane, and hold negative views of Louis Armstrong. Unsurprisingly, traditional jazz is mostly being kept alive by white (and Asian) musicians outside of Louisiana (for example, Woody Allen plays in a band that performs traditional Jazz).

So why do we abandon our music? Even in the rap world, songs that are only a few months old get pushed out of rotation for being "passe" or played out. Danny Barker's theory was: *"A negro don't wanna hear the music he heard five years ago. He's creative.*

He's always searching for something new, and he's trying to throw off what's been with his past because his past has been disgusting to him."[3]

This puts us in dangerous territory, because the story is much bigger than music. Take Egypt for example. White anthropologists have been debating on who built the pyramids for hundreds of years now. After their belief that the ancient Egyptians were white was disproven, they've given credit to Arabs, aliens, and any other entity besides Black Africans. The most credit they'll give us comes when they describe ancient Egypt as a multicultural place, where there was no such thing as race. This is true for Jazz as well, with many historians romanticizing post-bellum New Orleans as an interracial paradise. If whites can't claim something as theirs, they'll insist on sharing it. They'll use code words like "multicultural" or "American", and against this we must fight.

Anything Blacks do in America will be technically American. Jazz wouldn't be Jazz without Ragtime, Creole traditional songs, Negro Spirituals, Afro Latin music, or Black church music. Just because we have white managers, white fans, or use European instruments, doesn't mean we aren't making Black music. And us claiming what is rightfully ours doesn't mean that other races can't participate. But be clear: people have shed blood and died for this music. From the slaves at Congo Square to the hundreads of thousands of Blacks who were murdered and incarcerated during the Crack Era: this culture was built off of sacrifice. And there are some of us (this writer included) who will be damned if we keep letting others reap the benefits of things we sow.

NOTES

DNA Tests: The Newest Threat to Black Identity (AncestryDNA, 23andMe)

[1.] Autry, Curt. "Grandson says 'Loving' movie gets one key point wrong." *NBC12.Com,* NBC News, 2 Nov. 2016.

[2.] Andrews-Dyer, Helena. "The African American Museum chooses 'Loving' for its first film screening." *WashingtonPost.Com,* The Washington Post, 25 Oct. 2016.

[3.] Bringing Them Home. (2010). Australian Human Rights Commission, p.85.

[4.] Beresford, Quentin & Omaji, Paul. *Our State of Mind: Racial Planning and the Stolen Generations* Fremantle Arts Centre Press, 1998. Print.

[5.] *Who is Black in America?* CNN Productions, 9 Dec. 2012

[6.] Miles, William B. "Deeply Rooted: The Complex Equation of What Makes You Black." *Ebony.Com,* Ebony Media Operations, 30 May 2016

[7.] Harris, Aisha. "Black American versus African-American: Why I Prefer to be called black American." *Slate.Com,* The Slate Group, 29 Jul. 2014.

Black Music and Our Reluctance to Claim it

[1] Dominic James "Nick" LaRocca papers. *Tempo Magazine.*1936. *Hogan Jazz Archive*

[2] Ingrid Monson. *The African Diaspora: A Musical Perspective* Routledge, pg. 324, 2003. Print

[3] Danny Barker "Interview #1." *New Orleans Jazz Man and Raconteur,* GHB Records, 2015

[4] *Variety Magazine,* Nov. 1916, pg. 20, *Archive.Org.* Web 8 Jan 2018

[5] Jefferson, Margo. "Ripping Off Black Music." *Harper's Magazine,* Jan. 1973, pg. 40, *Archive.Org.* Web 8 Jan. 2018